DRAW
50
CATS

DRAW 50 CATS

LEE J. AMES

 DOUBLEDAY

NEW YORK   LONDON   TORONTO   SYDNEY   AUCKLAND

A MAIN STREET BOOK
PUBLISHED BY DOUBLEDAY
a division of Bantam Doubleday Dell Publishing Group, Inc.
1540 Broadway, New York, New York 10036

MAIN STREET BOOKS, DOUBLEDAY, and the portrayal of a
building with a tree are trademarks of Doubleday, a
division of Bantam Doubleday Dell Publishing Group, Inc.

Library of Congress Cataloging-in-Publication Data:
Ames, Lee J.
   Draw 50 cats.
   Summary: Step-by-step instructions on how to draw a variety of cats, including
domestic breeds, wild cats, cuddly kittens, and celebrity cats.
   1. Cats in art—Juvenile literature.   2. Drawing—Technique—Juvenile literature.
[1. Cats in art.   2. Drawing—Technique]   I. Title.   II. Title: Draw fifty cats.
NC780.A4818   1986   743'.6974428   86-8964
ISBN 0-385-23484-8
ISBN 0-385-23485-6 (lib. bdg.)
ISBN 0-385-24640-4 (pbk.)

Text and illustrations copyright © 1986 by Lee J. Ames and Murray D. Zak

Felix the Cat © 1986 Felix the Cat Productions, Inc., reprinted with special permission
of King Features Syndicate, Inc.
Morris, the 9 Lives® cat, © 1986 Star-Kist Foods, Inc., owner of the registered trademark, used with permission.
Miss Lil copyright © 1983 by Rick Detorie, used with permission.

This is for my lovely new grandkitten,
Lauren Michelle . . .

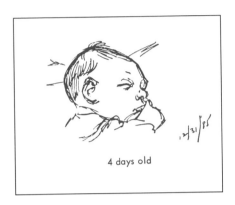

4 days old

Thanks, Warren, for all your help.

TO THE READER

This book will show you a way to draw a wide variety of your favorite felines. You need not start with the first illustration. Choose whichever you wish. When you have decided, follow the step-by-step method shown. *Very lightly* and *carefully,* sketch out step number one. However, this step, which is the easiest, should be done *most carefully.* Step number two is added right to step number one, also lightly and also very carefully. Step number three is sketched right on top of numbers one and two. Continue this way to the last step.

It may seem strange to ask you to be extra careful when you are drawing what seem to be the easiest first steps, but this is most important because a careless mistake at the beginning may spoil the whole picture at the end. As you sketch out each step, watch the spaces between the lines, as well as the lines, and see that they are the same. After each step, you may want to lighten your work by pressing it with a kneaded eraser (available at art supply stores).

When you have finished, you may want to redo the final step in India ink with a fine brush or pen. When the ink is dry, use the kneaded eraser to clean off the pencil lines. The eraser will not affect the India ink.

Here are some suggestions: In the first few steps, even when all seems quite correct, you might do well to hold your work up to a mirror. Sometimes the mirror shows that you've twisted the drawing off to one side without being aware of it. At first you may find it difficult to draw the boxes, triangles, or circles, or just to make the pencil go where you wish. Don't be discouraged. The more you practice, the more control you will develop. Use a compass or a ruler if you wish; professional artists do! The only equipment you'll need will be a medium or soft pencil, paper, the kneaded eraser and, if you wish, a compass, ruler, pen or brush.

The first steps in this book are shown darker than necessary so that they can be clearly seen. (Keep your own work very light.)

Remember, there are many other ways and methods to make drawings. This book shows just one method. Why don't you seek out other ways and methods to make drawings—from teachers, from libraries and, most important . . . from inside yourself?

LEE J. AMES

TO THE PARENT
OR TEACHER

"Leslie can draw a Siamese cat better than anybody else!" Such peer acclaim and encouragement generate incentive. Contemporary methods of art instruction (freedom of expression, experimentation, self-evaluation of competence and growth) provide a vigorous, fresh-air approach for which we must all be grateful.

New ideas need not, however, totally exclude the old. One such is the "follow me, step-by-step" approach. In my young learning days this method was so common, and frequently so exclusive, that the student became nothing more than a pantographic extension of the teacher. In those days it was excessively overworked.

This does not mean that the young hand is never to be guided. Rather, specific guiding is fundamental. Step-by-step guiding that produces satisfactory results is valuable even when the means of accomplishment are not fully understood by the student.

The novice with a musical instrument is frequently taught to play simple melodies as quickly as possible, well before he learns the most elemental scratchings at the surface of music theory. The resultant self-satisfaction, pride in accomplishment, can be a significant means of providing motivation. And all from mimicking an instructor's "Do-as-I-do . . ."

Mimicry is prerequisite for developing creativity. We learn the use of our tools by mimicry. Then we can use those tools for creativity. To this end I would offer the budding artist the opportunity to memorize or mimic (rote-like, if you wish) the making of "pictures." "Pictures" he has been anxious to be able to draw.

The use of this book should be available to anyone who *wants* to try another way of flapping his wings. Perhaps he or she will then get off the ground when a friend says, "Leslie can draw a Siamese cat better than anybody else!"

LEE J. AMES

DRAW
50
CATS

American Shorthair

Maine Coon

Persian

Rex

Manx

Egyptian Mau

Long-haired Tabby

Birman

Havana Brown

Abyssinian

Burmese

Seal Point Siamese

Calico

HEAD SHOTS AND PORTRAITS

WILD CATS
Jaguar

Cheetah

Leopard

Tiger

Bobcat

Caracal

Cougar

Lion

FAMOUS CATS
Morris, the 9 Lives® Cat
© 1986 Star-Kist Foods, Inc., owner of the registered trademark,
Morris, the 9 Lives® Cat. Used with permission.

Miss Lil

Puss in Boots

Fat Ferdie Freeloader

Felix the Cat
© 1986 Felix the Cat Productions, Inc.
FELIX THE CAT reprinted with special permission of King Features Syndicate, Inc.

KITTENS
Kitten takes its first steps.

Kittens are naturally curious.

Persian kitten

Kittens at play

COMMON BEHAVIOR
Offensive posture

Defensive posture

At play

A short snooze

Grooming

A curious Tabby

Courtship display

Frightened

Good night

DRAW 50 FOR HOURS OF FUN!

*Using Lee J. Ames's proven, step-by-step method of drawing instruction you can easily
learn to draw animals, monsters, airplanes, cars, sharks, buildings, dinosaurs, famous cartoons, and so much
more! Millions of people have learned to draw by using the award-winning
"Draw 50" technique. Now you can too!*

COLLECT THE ENTIRE DRAW 50 SERIES!

*The Draw 50 Series books are available from your local bookstore.
You may also order direct (make a copy of this form to order).*

Titles are paperback, unless otherwise indicated.

ISBN	TITLE	PRICE	QTY	TOTAL
23629-8	Airplanes, Aircraft, and Spacecraft	$8.00/$10.00 Can	X _____ =	_____
19519-2	Animals	$8.00/$10.00 Can	X _____ =	_____
24638-2	Athletes	$8.00/$10.00 Can	X _____ =	_____
26767-3	Beasties and Yugglies and Turnover Uglies and Things That Go Bump in the Night	$8.00/$10.00 Can	X _____ =	_____
24625-0	Beasties and Yugglies and Turnover Uglies and ThingsThat Go Bump in the Night (hardcover)	$12.95/$15.95 Can	X _____ =	_____
23630-1	Boats, Ships, Trucks and Trains	$8.00/$10.00 Can	X _____ =	_____
41777-2	Buildings and Other Structures	$8.00/$10.00 Can	X _____ =	_____
24639-0	Cars, Trucks and Motorcycles	$8.00/$10.00 Can	X _____ =	_____
24640-4	Cats	$8.00/$10.00 Can	X _____ =	_____
42449-3	Creepy Crawlies	$8.00/$10.00 Can	X _____ =	_____
41189-8	Creepy Crawlies (hardcover)	$12.95/$16.95 Can	X _____ =	_____
19520-6	Dinosaurs and Other Prehistoric Animals	$8.00/$10.00 Can	X _____ =	_____
23431-7	Dogs	$8.00/$10.00 Can	X _____ =	_____
46985-3	Endangered Animals	$8.00/$10.00 Can	X _____ =	_____
24629-3	Famous Caricatures (hardcover)	$12.95/$15.95 Can	X _____ =	_____
19521-4	Famous Cartoons	$8.00/$10.00 Can	X _____ =	_____
23432-5	Famous Faces	$8.00/$10.00 Can	X _____ =	_____
26770-3	Holiday Decorations	$8.00/$10.00 Can	X _____ =	_____
17642-2	Horses	$8.00/$10.00 Can	X _____ =	_____
17639-2	Monsters	$8.00/$10.00 Can	X _____ =	_____
41194-4	People (available 9/94)	$8.00/$10.50 Can	X _____ =	_____
26768-1	Sharks, Whales and Other Sea Creatures	$8.00/$10.00 Can	X _____ =	_____
47150-5	Flowers, Trees and Other Plants	$8.00/$10.50 Can	X _____ =	_____
47004-5	Flowers, Trees and Other Plants (hardcover)	$13.00/$16.95 Can	X _____ =	_____
14154-8	Vehicles	$8.00/$10.00 Can	X _____ =	_____
	Shipping and handling	**(add $2.50 per order)**	X _____ =	_____
		TOTAL		_____

*Please send me the title(s) I have indicated above. I am enclosing $_____.
Send check or money order in U.S. funds only (no C.O.D.s or cash, please). Make check payable to
Doubleday Consumer Services. Allow 4 - 6 weeks for delivery.
Prices and availability are subject to change without notice.*

Name:_____

Address:_____ Apt. # _____

City:_____ State:_____ ZIP Code: _____

Send completed coupon and payment to:

Doubleday Consumer Services
Dept. LA 18
2451 South Wolf Road
Des Plaines, IL 60018

MAIN STREET BOOKS

LA 18 – 2/95